CUSTARDS & PUDDINGS
The Ultimate Recipe Book

Sweet and Creamy
Custard and Pudding Recipes
For Beginners

Les Ilagan

Copyright © CONTENT ARCADE PUBLISHING

All rights reserved.

This recipe book is copyright protected and meant for personal use only. No part of this cookbook may be used, paraphrased, reproduced, scanned, distributed, or sold in any printed or electronic form without permission of the author and the publishing company. Copying pages or any part of this book for any purpose other than own personal use is prohibited and would also mean a violation of copyright law.

DISCLAIMER

Content Arcade Publishing and its authors are joined together in their efforts to create these pages and their publications. Content Arcade Publishing and its authors make no assurance of any kind, stated or implied, with respect to the information provided.

LIMITS OF LIABILITY

Content Arcade Publishing and its authors shall not be held legally responsible in the event of incidental or consequential damages in line with or arising out of, the supplying of the information presented here.

Table of Contents

Introduction i
Homemade Caramel Custard Pudding 1
Baked Custard Pudding with Maple 3
Caramelized Orange Cream Custard 5
Creamy Vanilla Custard with Caramel Sauce 7
Sweet Custard with Saffron 9
Mexican-Style Flan 11
Almond Caramel Custard 13
Baked Citrus Custard with Blueberry 15
Homemade Crème Brulee 17
Orange Pudding with White Chocolate Sauce 19
Creamy Pudding with Raspberry Sauce 21
Mango Vanilla Pudding with Maple 23
No-Cook Banana Vanilla Pudding 25
Silken Chocolate and Tofu Pudding 27
Pomegranate and Banana Pudding 29
Almond Strawberry Pudding 31
Creamy Pistachio Pudding 33
Deep Dark Chocolate Pudding with Whipped Cream .. 35
Creamy Banana Pudding with Sprinkles 37

Spiced Pumpkin and Vanilla Pudding Dessert............. 39
Vanilla Pudding with Blueberries............................... 41
Peach Banana and Orange Pudding........................... 43
Chocolate Avocado Pudding with Blueberries............. 45
Almond Choco and Banana Pudding 47
Ricotta Vanilla Pudding with Red Currants................. 49
Nutty Choco Pudding with Banana............................ 51
Vegan Avocado Banana and Choco Pudding 53
Mango Cream Pudding 55
Almond Panna Cotta with Fresh Fruits 57
Easy Mocha Pudding 59
Spiced Semolina Pudding with Sweet Cherries........... 61
Homemade Two Berry Semolina Pudding................... 63
Semolina Coconut Pudding with Raspberries 65
Chia Yogurt and Blueberry Pudding 67
Chia Pudding with Matcha Pomegranates and Almonds 68
Coco Chia Pudding with Mango 70
Apple Cinnamon and Oat Pudding with Chia.............. 72
Blueberry Chia Pudding with Maple 74
Strawberry and Chia Pudding with Granola 75
Persimmon Oat and Chia Pudding 77
Cardamom-Spiced Rice Pudding with Dried Cherry..... 79

Spiced Rice Pudding with Blueberries 81
Chocolate Rice Pudding with Cinnamon 83
Almond Rice Pudding with Figs 85
Mixed Berry Vanilla Rice Pudding 87
Spiced Rice Pudding with Raisins 89
Lemony Rice Pudding with Cinnamon 91
Vanilla Rice Pudding with Warm Cherry Sauce 93
Creamy Rice Pudding with Apple and Cinnamon 95
Spiced Almond Rice Pudding..................................... 97
Yummy Orange Pudding 99
Sweet Lemon Pudding Cake 101
Bread Pudding with Cranberry and Caramel Sauce ...103
Bread Pudding with Raisins and Walnuts 105

Introduction

Who wouldn't want to have a sweet, silky, and creamy dessert that melts in your mouth and makes you crave for more? If you are looking for a delectable sweet treat, this book will surely provide for you! It covers many rich and creamy custard recipes as well as silky pudding recipes.

Making your own fabulous dessert does not require much cooking skills, by simply following the recipe instructions in this book, you can easily make something that will satisfy your sweet tooth.

This book contains beginner-friendly instructions, easy to find ingredients, and just the right combination of flavors to delight your taste buds.

We all know that a sumptuous meal will not be complete without having a sweet and creamy dessert. This book offers a wonderful selection of mouth-watering custard and pudding recipes that will satisfy your every sweet craving.

This book is a part of many cookbook series that I am writing; I hope that you'll enjoy all the recipes here.

Homemade Caramel Custard Pudding

Preparation Time: 15 minutes
Total Time: 5 hours 15 minutes
Yield: 10 servings

Ingredients

For the Caramel Sauce:
1/4 cup (60 ml) water
1 cup (220 g) light brown sugar

For the Custard:
8 (20 g) egg yolks
4 (60 g) whole eggs
1 (14.5 fl. oz. or 406 ml) can evaporated milk
1 (14 fl. oz. or 397 ml) can condensed milk
1 tsp. (5 ml) pure vanilla extract

You will need:
4 custard or flan mold pans
steamer
water for the steamer

Method

1. Combine water and sugar in a small pot or saucepan. Bring to a boil over medium-high heat. Lower heat to medium-low. Cook until the sugar

caramelizes and becomes golden brown in color. Do not to overcook or else your caramel will taste bitter. Pour the caramel to the custard mold pans and spread evenly. Set aside.
2. Fill your steamer with just enough amount of water and bring to a boil over medium heat.
3. Meanwhile, combine together the yolks, eggs, sweetened condensed milk, evaporated milk, and vanilla extract in a large bowl. Stir gently until blended well. Strain the mixture into the prepared custard mold pans. Cover with foil and then put in the steamer.

    Note: Make sure to let it boil first before you put them in. Cover with lid. Reduce heat to low and steam until the custard is firm, about 40-45 minutes. Set aside to cool at room temperature, then refrigerate for at least 4 hours or until ready to serve.
4. Run a knife along the sides of each custard to loosen them up. Invert onto serving plates.
5. Serve and enjoy.

Nutritional Information:
Energy - 280 calories
Fat - 0.0 g
Carbohydrates - 37.2 g
Protein - 9.3 g
Sodium - 114 mg

Baked Custard Pudding with Maple

Preparation Time: 15 minutes
Total Time: 5 hours 15 minutes
Yield: 8 servings

Ingredients

For the Caramel Sauce:
1/4 cup (60 ml) water
3/4 cup (165 g) brown sugar
1/4 cup (60 g) maple syrup

For the Custard:
5 (60 g) whole eggs
8 (20 g) egg yolks
2 cups (500 ml) whole milk
1 can (14 fl. oz. or 397 ml) sweetened condensed milk
1 tsp. (5 ml) pure vanilla extract

Method

1. Preheat your oven and set it to 350 F (175).
2. Combine water, brown sugar, and 1/4 cup maple syrup in a saucepan. Bring to a boil over medium-high heat. Lower heat to medium-low. Cook until the sugar caramelizes and becomes golden brown in color. Pour into eight (3.5-ounce)

ramekins and evenly spread the caramel. Set aside.
3. Whisk together the eggs in a bowl until lightly beaten. Stir in whole milk, sweetened condensed milk, and vanilla extract until incorporated. Pour the custard mixture over caramel.
4. Place the ramekins in a baking dish. Pour just enough water into the baking dish to cover ramekins halfway up the sides.
5. Bake in the oven for about 40-45 minutes or until a skewer inserted in the center of the custard comes out clean. Remove from heat. Take out the ramekins from the baking dish and cool at room temperature.
6. Chill for 4 hours before serving. Invert each ramekin onto individual plates.
7. Serve and enjoy.

Nutritional Information:
Energy - 297 calories
Fat - 9.8 g
Carbohydrates - 44.1 g
Protein - 9.1 g
Sodium - 113 mg

Caramelized Orange Cream Custard

Preparation Time: 15 minutes
Total Time: 5 hours 15 minutes
Yield: 10 servings

Ingredients

For the Caramel:
3 Tbsp. (45 ml) water
1 cup (220 g) light brown sugar
1 1/2 tsp. (5 g) orange zest, finely grated

For the Custard:
8 (20 g) egg yolks
4 (60 g) whole eggs
1 (14 fl. oz. or 397 ml) can condensed milk
1 (14.5 fl. oz. or 406 ml) can evaporated milk
1 tsp. (5 ml) orange extract
water, for the steamer

Method

1. Bring water and brown sugar to a boil in a saucepan. Reduce the heat to low, then add the orange zest. Cook until the sugar caramelizes and golden brown in color. Make sure not to

overcook or else your caramel will give you a bitter taste. Pour the caramel into 10 (3.5-ounce) custard mold pans or ramekins and spread the caramel evenly. Set aside.
2. Fill the bottom part of your steamer with just enough water. Cover and bring to a boil over medium flame.
3. Combine the eggs, condensed milk, evaporated milk, and orange extract in a large bowl. Strain the mixture into the prepared custard mold pans. Cover with foil and put them in the steamer.
4. Check if the water is boiling before you put them in. Cover with lid. Reduce heat to low and steam until the custard is firm, about 40-45 minutes. Let cool at room temperature, then chill for at least 4 hours.
5. Loosen them up by running a knife at the sides. Invert into serving plates.
6. Serve and enjoy!

Nutritional Information:
Energy - 259 calories
Fat - 10.8 g
Carbohydrates - 32.1 g
Protein - 9.3 g
Sodium - 112 mg

Creamy Vanilla Custard with Caramel Sauce

Preparation Time: 15 minutes
Total Time: 5 hours 15 minutes
Yield: 10 servings

Ingredients

For the Caramel:
3 Tbsp. (45 ml) water
1 cup (220 g) light brown sugar

For the Custard:
1 (14 fl. oz. or 397 ml) can sweetened condensed milk
2 cups (500 ml) whole milk
1 cup (250 g) heavy cream
2/3 cup (150 g) white sugar
6 (60 g) whole eggs
1 tsp. (5 ml) pure vanilla extract

Method

1. Preheat your oven and set it to 350 F (175).
2. In a small non-stick saucepan, heat the water and sugar over medium flame. Shake and swirl occasionally to evenly distribute the sugar until it is dissolved completely and begins to brown. Remove from the heat source and continue to brown the sugar until it becomes dark golden

brown. Pour the caramelized sugar into 10 (3.5-ounce) custard or flan molds and coat evenly the base.
3. In a large bowl, whisk together the sweetened condensed milk, whole milk, cream, eggs, and vanilla. Pour over the caramelized sugar.
4. Place the filled custard molds into a large baking dish and add about an inch of hot water to the baking dish. Bake in the preheated oven for about 40-45 minutes, or until set. Let cool at room temperature, and then chill for 4 hours.
5. Serve and enjoy.

Nutritional Information:
Energy - 311 calories
Fat - 11.5 g
Carbohydrates - 45.2 g
Protein - 8.3 g
Sodium - 118 mg

Sweet Custard with Saffron

Preparation Time: 10 minutes
Total Time: 4 hours 45 minutes
Yield: 4 servings

Ingredients

2 cups (500 ml) whole milk
pinch of saffron threads
2 Tbsp. (15 g) corn flour
2 (60 g) whole eggs, lightly beaten
1/4 cup (25 g) powdered sugar
2 Tbsp. (40 ml) honey
1 tsp. (2 g) cinnamon, ground

Method

1. Combine the milk and saffron in a pot or saucepan and bring to a simmer over medium flame. Remove from heat and set aside to infuse for about 30 minutes.
2. Place the corn flour in a large bowl, then add a small amount of the cooled milk to dilute the corn flour; whisk until smooth.
3. Stir in the eggs and sugar. Mix well. Pour mixture into the saucepan with the remaining milk; cook over medium flame, stirring continuously until thick and smooth. Remove from heat, stir in the

honey, and then divide mixture evenly among four ramekins and cover with plastic wrap. Chill for at least 4 hours or until ready to serve.
4. Sprinkle with some ground cinnamon on top before serving.
5. Serve and enjoy.

Nutritional Information:
Energy - 180 calories
Fat - 6.3 g
Carbohydrates - 25.1 g
Protein - 7.0 g
Sodium - 80 mg

Mexican-Style Flan

Preparation Time: 15 minutes
Total Time: 5 hours 15 minutes
Yield: 10 servings

Ingredients

3/4 cup (165 g) white sugar
3 Tbsp. (45 ml) water
2 tsp. (7 g) orange peel (grated)
1 cup (250 ml) whole milk
1 cup (250 ml) heavy cream
1 (14 fl. oz. or 397 ml) can sweetened condensed milk
4 (60 g) whole eggs
8 (20 g) egg yolks
1/4 cup (60 ml) fresh orange juice
1 tsp. (5 ml) vanilla extract
1 Tbsp. (7 g) cornstarch

Method

1. Place the sugar, water, and orange peel in a heavy-bottomed saucepan over medium heat. Cook until the sugar is dissolved and turns a golden amber in color, about 7 minutes. Watch closely once the syrup begins to change color because it can burn easily. Remove from heat. Pour the sugar syrup into 10 (3.5-ounce) flan molds or ramekins. Set aside to cool.

2. Preheat your oven and set it to 350 F (175).
3. Mix together the whole milk, cream, sweetened condensed milk, eggs, orange juice, vanilla extract, and cornstarch in a large bowl until smooth. Strain mixture over the cooled caramel syrup in the flan molds.
4. Place the flan molds inside a large baking dish. Fill the baking dish with boiling water to reach halfway up the sides of the flan molds.
5. Bake in the oven until the middle of the flan is firm but still slightly jiggly when moved, about 45 minutes. Allow the flan cool, then chill for 4 hours.
6. To serve, run a knife around the sides to loosen the flan. Invert a plate on the mold, then turn the mold over, and carefully unmold the flan with the syrupy caramel topping.
7. Serve and enjoy.

Nutritional Information:
Energy - 315 calories
Fat - 14.1 g
Carbohydrates - 40.2 g
Protein - 8.6 g
Sodium - 96 mg

Almond Caramel Custard

Preparation Time: 15 minutes
Total Time: 5 hours 15 minutes
Yield: 8 servings

Ingredients
1 cup (220 g) white sugar
1/4 cup (60 ml) water
1 (14.5 fl. oz. or 406 ml) can evaporated milk
1 (14 fl. oz. or 397 ml) can sweetened condensed milk
5 (60 g) whole eggs
6 (20 g) egg yolks
2 tsp. (10 ml) almond extract
thinly sliced banana, to serve (optional)
chocolate shavings, to serve (optional)

Method
1. Preheat your oven and set it to 350 F (175).
2. In a heavy saucepan over medium heat, cook sugar with water until dissolved and golden brown. Pour into eight (3.5-ounce) flan molds or ramekins, tilting to coat the base. Set aside.
3. In a large bowl, mix together the evaporated milk, condensed milk, eggs, and almond extract. Try not to incorporate any air into the custard

mixture. Pour into prepared ramekins, and tap lightly on the counter to remove any bubbles.
4. Place the ramekins inside a large baking dish. Fill the baking dish with boiling water to reach halfway up the sides of the flan molds.
5. Bake in the oven until the middle of the flan is firm but still slightly jiggly when moved, about 45 minutes. Allow the custard to cool, then chill for 4 hours.
6. To serve, run a knife around the sides to loosen the custard. Invert a plate on the mold, turn the mold over, and carefully unmold the custard with caramel syrup.
7. Top with banana slices and chocolate shavings.
8. Serve and enjoy.

Nutritional Information:
Energy - 338 calories
Fat - 12.9 g
Carbohydrates - 45.0 g
Protein - 11.7 g
Sodium - 142 mg

Baked Citrus Custard with Blueberry

Preparation Time: 15 minutes
Total Time: 5 hours 15 minutes
Yield: 6 servings

Ingredients

1 cup (220 g) granulated sugar
1/3 cup (40 g) all-purpose flour
1/4 tsp. salt
2 cups (500 ml) skim milk
4 (20 g) egg yolks, lightly beaten
1/4 cup (60 ml) lemon juice
1 1/2 tsp. (5 g) lemon zest, finely grated
4 (40 g) egg whites
1/2 cup (75 g) blueberries
fresh mint sprigs, for garnish

Method

1. Preheat your oven and set it to 350 F (175).
2. Mix together the granulated sugar, all-purpose flour, and salt together in a bowl.
3. Stir in milk, egg yolks, lemon juice, and lemon zest until smooth.
4. Beat egg whites in a bowl until stiff peaks form. Fold in egg whites into the flour mixture until blended well. Pour into a 1-quart (950 L) baking dish.

5. Place the baking dish in a larger size baking pan. Pour water into baking pan to make a 1-inch deep water bath around the baking dish.
6. Bake in the oven until set in the middle, about 50 minutes to an hour. Allow to cool and chill for 4 hours or until ready to serve.
7. Top with blueberries and garnish with fresh mint sprigs.
8. Serve and enjoy.

Nutritional Information:
Energy - 258 calories
Fat - 3.4 g
Carbohydrates - 50.5 g
Protein - 8.1 g
Sodium - 170 mg

Homemade Crème Brulee

Preparation Time: 10 minutes
Total Time: 5 hours
Yield: 5 servings

Ingredients

6 (20 g) egg yolks
8 Tbsp. (110 g) granulated sugar, divided
1 tsp. (5 ml) pure vanilla extract
2 1/2 cups (375 ml) half and half cream
2 Tbsp. (30 g) brown sugar
fresh blueberries, to serve
mint leaves, for garnish

Method

1. Preheat your oven and set it to 350 F (175).
2. In a medium pot or saucepan, mix together the egg yolks, 6 tablespoons of granulated sugar, and vanilla extract until blended well. Cook over a low flame, stirring constantly until almost boiling. Remove from heat.
3. Stir in the cream. Mix well.
4. Pour the cream mixture into the top part of a double boiler. Fill the bottom part with just enough water and bring to a simmer over

medium flame, stirring constantly for 3-5 minutes. Remove mixture from the heat source and divide among five ramekins.
5. Bake in the oven for about 40-45 minutes. Allow to cool at room temperature, then chill for 4 hours or until ready to serve.
6. Combine the remaining white sugar and brown sugar in a small bowl and then sprinkle this mixture on top of each custard.
7. With a kitchen blow torch, caramelize the sugar. Top with a few berries and garnish with mint leaves.
8. Serve and enjoy.

Nutritional Information:
Energy - 325 calories
Fat - 19.4 g
Carbohydrates - 32.9 g
Protein - 7.0 g
Sodium - 61 mg

Orange Pudding with White Chocolate Sauce

Preparation Time: 10 minutes
Total Time: 4 hours 40 minutes
Yield: 8 servings

Ingredients

1 cup (250 ml) fresh orange juice
1/2 cup (110 g) granulated sugar
2 cups (500 ml) milk
1 cup (250 g) heavy cream
3/4 cup (225 ml) sweetened condensed milk
1/3 cup (35 g) cornstarch
3 oz. (85 g) melted white chocolate chips, to serve
1 medium (140 g) orange, cut into wedges

Method

1. In a medium saucepan, bring the orange juice to a boil along with the granulated sugar over medium flame.
2. Whisk together the cornstarch and 1 cup milk in a large bowl until dissolved completely. Stir in the remaining milk, heavy cream, and sweetened condensed milk. Mix well. Add this mixture into the saucepan with the orange juice. Cook, stirring

constantly until the mixture becomes thickened. Remove from heat.
3. Divide the orange pudding mixture equally among eight (3.5-ounce) ramekins or flan molds. Let cool and chill for at least 4 hours covered with plastic wrap.
4. Invert pudding onto individual plates, and then drizzle with melted white chocolate. Garnish with orange wedges.
5. Serve and enjoy.

Nutritional Information:
Energy - 324 calories
Fat - 12.8 g
Carbohydrates - 48.6 g
Protein - 5.6 g
Sodium - 81 mg

Creamy Pudding with Raspberry Sauce

Preparation Time: 20 minutes
Total Time: 4 hours 20 minutes
Yield: 6 servings

Ingredients
2 cups (250 g) fresh raspberries, divided
3/4 cup (165 g) sugar, divided
1/3 cup (35 g) cornstarch
2 cups (500 ml) whole milk
1 cup (250 g) heavy cream

Method
1. Place 1 cup of raspberries in a food processor and puree. Pour into a small saucepan. Add 1/4 cup sugar and the remaining raspberries. Cook, stirring occasionally for about 8-10 minutes over medium flame. Remove from heat, and let cool. Cover and keep in the fridge until it is ready to use.
2. In a separate saucepan, mix together the milk and cornstarch until dissolved. Cook over medium flame, stirring often until thickened.
3. Stir in cream and the remaining 1/2 cup sugar. Heat for a few minutes until heated through, and

the sugar has been dissolved completely. Pour among six ramekins, dividing the mixture evenly between them.
4. Let cool, and then chill for at least 4 hours. Invert each mold onto individual serving plates. Top with prepared raspberry sauce.
5. Serve and enjoy.

Nutritional Information:
Energy - 324 calories
Fat - 10.2 g
Carbohydrates - 57.5 g
Protein - 3.6 g
Sodium - 42 mg

Mango Vanilla Pudding with Maple

Preparation Time: 10 minutes
Total Time: 2 hours 20 minutes
Yield: 8 servings

Ingredients
1/2 cup (110 g) brown sugar
1/4 cup (80 ml) maple syrup
1/4 cup (60 ml) water
1 cup (165 g) fresh mangoes, diced
2 1/2 cups (625 ml) whole milk
1/3 cup (35 g) cornstarch
1 cup (250 g) heavy cream
1/2 cup (150 ml) sweetened condensed milk

Method
1. In a medium saucepan, bring the brown sugar, maple syrup, and water to a boil over medium heat. Add the mangoes and cook for about 10 minutes. Remove from heat, and allow to cool.
2. Whisk together 1 cup milk and cornstarch in a large bowl until dissolved completely. Stir in the remaining milk, heavy cream, and sweetened condensed milk. Mix well. Cook over medium flame, stirring constantly until the mixture thickens. Remove from heat.

3. Divide the pudding mixture evenly among eight ramekins or flan molds. Let cool and then place in the chiller for at least 4 hours to set.
4. Invert pudding onto individual dessert bowls. Top with mangoes and sauce.
5. Serve and enjoy.

Nutritional Information:
Energy - 257 calories
Fat - 9.0 g
Carbohydrates - 41.2 g
Protein - 4.7 g
Sodium - 70 mg

No-Cook Banana Vanilla Pudding

Preparation Time: 10 minutes
Total Time: 4 hours 20 minutes
Yield: 8 servings

Ingredients

4 oz. (125 g) cream cheese, softened
1 (3.5 oz. or 100 g) package instant vanilla pudding mix
1 (3.5 oz. or 100 g) package instant banana pudding mix
1 can (14 fl. oz. or 397 ml) sweetened condensed milk
3 cups (750 ml) whole milk, cold
1/2 cup (125 g) sour cream
1/2 cup (125 g) whipped cream
3 (120 g) medium bananas, thinly sliced

Method

1. Using an electric mixer, beat the cream cheese in a large bowl until smooth. Add the pudding mixes, sweetened condensed milk, cold milk, and sour cream. Mix until smooth.
2. Fold the whipped cream into pudding mixture. Divide evenly among eight dessert cups and top with banana slices. Cover and then chill for at least 4 hours to set.
3. Serve and enjoy.

Nutritional Information:
Energy - 311 calories
Fat - 13.1 g
Carbohydrates - 41.4 g
Protein - 8.3 g
Sodium - 185 mg

Silken Chocolate and Tofu Pudding

Preparation Time: 10 minutes
Total Time: 4 hours 20 minutes
Yield: 6 servings

Ingredients

1 cup (160 g) semisweet chocolate chips
1/4 cup (60 g) heavy cream
1 (16 oz. or 450 g) package firm tofu, drained
1 cup (250 ml) soy milk, warmed
1 tsp. (5 ml) pure vanilla extract

Method

1. Melt the chocolate in a heavy saucepan or double boiler.
2. Using a blender or food processor, combine tofu, melted chocolate, soymilk, and vanilla extract. Process until the mixture becomes smooth. Divide equally among six dessert cups. Cover and then chill for at least 4 hours to set.
3. Serve and enjoy.

Nutritional Information:
Energy - 281 calories
Fat - 16.4 g
Carbohydrates - 28.1 g
Protein - 7.6 g
Sodium - 32 mg

Pomegranate and Banana Pudding

Preparation Time: 10 minutes
Total Time: 4 hours 20 minutes
Yield: 8 servings

Ingredients

1 (3.5 oz. or 100 g) package instant vanilla pudding mix
1 (3.5 oz. or 100 g) package instant banana pudding mix
2/3 cup (200 ml) sweetened condensed milk
3 cups (750 ml) skim milk, cold
1/2 cup (125 g) whipping cream
2 cups (360 g) pomegranate seeds
2 (120 g) medium bananas, thinly sliced

Method

4. Using an electric mixer, combine the pudding mixes, sweetened condensed milk, cold milk, and cream. Mix together until blended well.
5. Fold in 1 cup of pomegranate seeds and bananas into pudding mixture.
6. Divide evenly among eight dessert glasses. Top with remaining pomegranate seeds. Cover and then chill for at least 4 hours to set.
7. Serve and enjoy.

Nutritional Information:
Energy - 303 calories
Fat – 6.7 g
Carbohydrates – 56.2 g
Protein - 5.9 g
Sodium - 336 mg

Almond Strawberry Pudding

Preparation Time: 10 minutes
Total Time: 4 hours 20 minutes
Yield: 8 servings

Ingredients

2 cups (400 g) strawberries, hulled and sliced
1 (1 oz. or 28 g) package strawberry flavored gelatin powder
2 (3 oz. or 85 g) packages instant vanilla pudding
4 cups (1 L) almond milk

Strawberry Sauce with Rosewater:
1 ½ cups (300 g) strawberries, hulled and chopped
1 cup (220 g) white sugar
3 Tbsp. (45 ml) water
2 tsp. (10 ml) rosewater

Method

1. Puree strawberries in a food processor. Transfer the strawberry puree into a saucepan and add the gelatin powder. Cook over medium flame for 3-5 minutes, stirring often. Remove from heat. Cool slightly.
2. Beat together the vanilla pudding and almond milk until it thickens.

3. Add the gelatin mixture and mix well. Pour into eight gelatin molds or ramekins. Cover and chill for 4 hours or until completely set.
4. Meanwhile, prepare the strawberry sauce by combining the chopped strawberries, white sugar, and rosewater. Bring to a boil over medium-high flame. Then, reduce the heat and simmer for 10 minutes. Stir in rosewater. Let cool.
5. Serve the pudding in individual plates with prepared strawberry sauce. Garnish with strawberry halves, if desired.
6. Enjoy.

Nutritional Information:

Energy - 259 calories

Fat - 1.7 g

Carbohydrates - 53.4 g

Protein - 10.3 g

Sodium - 203 mg

Creamy Pistachio Pudding

Preparation Time: 10 minutes
Total Time: 4 hours 20 minutes
Yield: 4 servings

Ingredients

Pistachio Paste:
1/2 cup (75 g) pistachio nuts, salted
1/3 cup (75 g) granulated sugar
2 Tbsp. (30 ml) water

Pudding:
2 cups (500 ml) whole milk
2 (60 g) egg yolks
1/3 cup (75 g) granulated sugar
1/4 cup (25 g) cornstarch
1/4 tsp. (1.5 g) salt
1 tsp. (5 ml) pure vanilla extract
2 Tbsp. (30 ml) unsalted butter, softened
1/2 cup (75 g) pistachio nuts, chopped

Method

1. Place pistachios in a food processor. Process until finely chopped. Add the sugar and water; blend until smooth.

2. Transfer the pistachio paste into a medium saucepan. Stir in milk and cook over medium heat until steamy and heated through
3. Meanwhile, whisk together granulated sugar, egg yolks, cornstarch, and salt. Keep mixing until smooth and thick. Pour in 1/2 cup of the hot pistachio milk into the sugar and egg mixture. Mix well. Add another half cup of steamed milk and whisk to combine well. Return this egg mixture into the saucepan. Cook, stirring over medium flame until thick and bubbly. Let it boil for about 1 minute, or until it becomes thickened. Remove from heat. Stir in butter and vanilla extract until the butter is melted. Strain mixture in a fine-mesh strainer placed over a medium glass bowl. Cool slightly.
4. Ladle into four flan molds or ramekins and cover with plastic wrap. Keep refrigerated for at least 4 hours to set.
5. Top with chopped pistachios.
6. Serve and enjoy.

Nutritional Information:
Energy - 321 calories
Fat - 15.7 g
Carbohydrates - 38.4 g
Protein - 7.8 g
Sodium - 254 mg

Deep Dark Chocolate Pudding with Whipped Cream

Preparation Time: 10 minutes
Total Time: 1 hour 20 minutes
Yield: 2 servings

Ingredients

1 cup (250 ml) whole milk
4 oz. (120 g) dark chocolate, melted
3 Tbsp. (45 g) brown sugar
1 Tbsp. (7 g) cornstarch
1 tsp. (5 ml) vanilla extract
whipped cream (optional)

Method

1. Combine the milk, chocolate, sugar, cornstarch, and vanilla extract in a small saucepan over low heat. Mix well until thick and smooth, about 10 minutes. Divide among two dessert cups or ramekins. Chill for at least an hour. Top with some whipped cream.
2. Serve and enjoy.

Nutritional Information:
Energy - 369 calories
Fat - 16.2 g
Carbohydrates - 46.6 g
Protein - 9.2 g
Sodium - 122 mg

Creamy Banana Pudding with Sprinkles

Preparation Time: 20 minutes
Total Time: 4 hours 20 minutes
Yield: 12 servings

Ingredients
1 (5 oz. or 150 g) package instant vanilla pudding mix
2 cups (500 ml) cold milk
1 cup (300 ml) sweetened condensed milk
2 tsp. (10 ml) vanilla extract
1 (12 oz. or 336 g) container - frozen whipped topping, thawed
8 (120 g) bananas, sliced
candy sprinkles, for topping (optional)

Method
1. In a large mixing bowl, beat the pudding mix and milk for 2 to 3 minutes using an electric mixer.
2. Add the condensed milk, vanilla extract, and whipped topping. Mix until well-blended.
3. Divide the banana slices among twelve ramekins or dessert cups. Top with pudding mixture. Cover and then chill for at least 4 hours to set.
4. Sprinkle with candy sprinkles if desired.
5. Serve and enjoy.

Nutritional Information:
Energy - 282 calories
Fat – 9.6 g
Carbohydrates – 45.9 g
Protein – 5.0 g
Sodium - 259 mg

Spiced Pumpkin and Vanilla Pudding Dessert

Preparation Time: 20 minutes
Total Time: 4 hours 20 minutes
Yield: 8 servings

Ingredients

1 (5 oz. or 150 g) package instant vanilla pudding mix
2 cups (500 ml) cold milk
1 cup (250 g) pumpkin puree
1/2 cup (150 ml) sweetened condensed milk
1/2 cup (125 ml) heavy cream
1 tsp. (2 g) cinnamon (ground)
whipped cream, to serve
ground nutmeg, to serve

Method

1. In a large mixing bowl, beat together the instant pudding and cold milk for 2 to 3 minutes using an electric mixer.
2. Add the pumpkin puree, condensed milk, cream, and cinnamon. Mix until smooth and blended well.
3. Divide the pudding mixture evenly among eight dessert cups. Cover and then chill for 4 hours to set.

4. Top with whipped cream and sprinkle with nutmeg.
5. Serve and enjoy.

Nutritional Information:
Energy - 301 calories
Fat - 12.8 g
Carbohydrates - 39.9 g
Protein - 9.0 g
Sodium - 217 mg

Vanilla Pudding with Blueberries

Preparation Time: 15 minutes
Total Time: 4 hours 15 minutes
Yield: 4 servings

Ingredients

3 cups (375 ml) whole milk
1/4 cup (55 g) white sugar
3 Tbsp. (20 g) cornstarch
1/4 tsp. (1.5 g) salt
1 tsp. (5 ml) pure vanilla extract
2 Tbsp. (30 g) unsalted butter
2 cups (300 g) blueberries

Method

1. Combine the milk, white sugar, cornstarch, and salt in a medium saucepan. Stir until completely dissolved. Cook over medium heat until the pudding mixture is thick enough to coat the back of a metal spoon. Turn off the heat.
2. Stir in vanilla extract and butter. Then, pour into four gelatin or flan molds. Cover and then chill for at least 4 hours to set.
3. Serve with blueberries and enjoy.

Nutritional Information:
Energy - 201 calories
Fat - 5.6 g
Carbohydrates - 34.6 g
Protein - 4.6 g
Sodium - 226 mg

Peach Banana and Orange Pudding

Preparation Time: 30 minutes
Total Time: 2 hours 30 minutes
Yield: 8 servings

Ingredients

3 (150 g) peaches, peeled and cut into small pieces
3 (120 g) banana, peeled and thinly sliced
4 cups (1 L) whole milk
3/4 cup (165 g) white sugar
3/4 cup (90 g) all-purpose flour
6 (20 g) egg yolks, beaten
1/4 cup (60 ml) fresh orange juice

Method

1. Divide peaches and bananas among eight dessert cups.
2. Mix together the milk, sugar, all-purpose flour, and beaten egg yolks in a medium saucepan. Cook over medium-low heat, stirring often until it thickens. Remove from the heat source and stir in the orange juice.
3. Divide the pudding mixture and spoon over the fruits. Let cool.
4. Cover and then chill for at least 4 hours to set.

5. Serve and enjoy.

Nutritional Information:
Energy - 298 calories
Fat - 7.8 g
Carbohydrates - 49.8 g
Protein - 8.9 g
Sodium - 65 mg

Chocolate Avocado Pudding with Blueberries

Preparation Time: 10 minutes
Total Time: 4 hours 10 minutes
Yield: 5 servings

Ingredients

2 (200 g) avocados, peeled and cut into small cubes
1/3 cup (35 g) unsweetened cocoa powder
1/3 cup (85 ml) skim milk
1/2 cup (110 g) brown sugar
2 tsp. (10 ml) vanilla extract
1/4 tsp. ground cinnamon
1 cup (150 g) blueberries
fresh mint, for garnish

Method

1. Combine the avocados, cocoa, skim milk, brown sugar, vanilla extract, and cinnamon in a blender. Process until smooth. Divide evenly among five dessert cups. Cover and then chill until firm, about 4 hours.
2. Top with some blueberries and garnish with fresh mint.
3. Serve and enjoy.

Nutritional Information:
Energy - 328 calories
Fat - 21.1 g
Carbohydrates - 36.9 g
Protein - 4.3 g
Sodium - 23 mg

Almond Choco and Banana Pudding

Preparation Time: 10 minutes
Total Time: 4 hours 20 minutes
Yield: 4 servings

Ingredients

2 cups (500 ml) almond milk, unsweetened
4 oz. (125 g) bittersweet chocolate, melted
2 Tbsp. (40 g) almond butter
3 Tbsp. (45 g) light brown sugar
2 Tbsp. (7 g) cornstarch
1 Tbsp. (15 g) butter
2 (120 g) banana, thinly sliced
1/2 cup (60 g) dry roasted almonds, chopped
1/4 cup (30 g) cacao nibs

Method

1. Combine the almond milk, melted chocolate, almond butter, sugar, and cornstarch in a small saucepan. Cook over a low flame, mixing well until thick and smooth, about 5-7 minutes. Cool slightly.
2. Fold in half of the chopped almonds and cacao nibs.

3. Divide evenly among four dessert cups or ramekins.
4. Cover and then chill for at least 4 hours to set. Top with banana slices and remaining almonds.
5. Serve and enjoy.

Nutritional Information:
Energy - 389 calories
Fat - 22.1 g
Carbohydrates - 48.6 g
Protein – 6.2 g
Sodium - 100 mg

Ricotta Vanilla Pudding with Red Currants

Preparation Time: 25 minutes
Total Time: 4 hours 25 minutes
Yield: 5 servings

Ingredients
2 1/2 cups (625 ml) whole milk
1/4 tsp. (1.5 g) salt
2 1/2 Tbsp. (18 g) cornstarch
1/2 cup (125 ml) cold water
1 cup (220 g) ricotta cheese
1/3 cup (115 ml) honey
1/4 tsp. (1.5 ml) vanilla extract
2 cups (240 g) red currants

Method
1. Mix together the milk and salt in a saucepan over medium heat, and bring to a boil.
2. Combine cornstarch and cold water in a small bowl. Mix until dissolved.
3. When the milk begins to boil, add the slurry (cornstarch mixture). Cook, stirring until it thickens, about 4-5 minutes.
4. Remove from heat and stir in the ricotta cheese, honey, and vanilla extract. Mix well.

5. Divide evenly among five dessert cups or ramekins. Cover and then chill for at least 4 hours to set.
6. Top with some red currants.
7. Serve and enjoy.

Nutritional Information:
Energy - 251 calories
Fat - 8.0 g
Carbohydrates - 36.5 g
Protein - 10.3 g
Sodium - 210 mg

Nutty Choco Pudding with Banana

Preparation Time: 10 minutes
Total Time: 4 hours 20 minutes
Yield: 4 servings

Ingredients

2 cups (500 ml) almond milk, unsweetened
4 oz. (125 g) dark chocolate, melted
2 Tbsp. (40 g) almond butter
3 Tbsp. (45 g) brown sugar
2 Tbsp. (7 g) cornstarch
1 tsp. (5 ml) vanilla extract
2 (120 g) banana, thinly sliced
1/2 cup (60 g) dry roasted almonds, chopped

Method

1. Whisk together almond milk, melted chocolate, almond butter, brown sugar, cornstarch, and vanilla extract in a small saucepan. Cook over low heat, mixing well until thick and smooth, about 5-7 minutes.
2. Divide evenly among four dessert cups or ramekins.
3. Cover and then chill for at least 4 hours to set. Top with banana slices and chopped almonds.
4. Serve and enjoy.

Nutritional Information:
Energy - 274 calories
Fat - 14.6 g
Carbohydrates - 32.9 g
Protein - 5.6 g
Sodium - 80 mg

Vegan Avocado Banana and Choco Pudding

Preparation Time: 10 minutes
Total Time: 4 hours 10 minutes
Yield: 5 servings

Ingredients

2 (200 g) avocados, peeled and cut into small cubes
2 (120 g) bananas, peeled and cut into small cubes
1/4 cup (25 g) unsweetened cocoa powder, plus more for garnish
1/2 cup (125 ml) soy milk
1 tsp. (10 ml) vanilla extract

Method

1. Combine the avocados, banana, cocoa powder, soy milk, and vanilla extract in a blender. Process until smooth. Divide evenly among five small dessert glasses. Cover and then chill for at least 4 hours to set.
2. Sprinkle with some cocoa powder.
3. Serve and enjoy.

Nutritional Information:
Energy - 231 calories
Fat – 16.8 g
Carbohydrates – 21.8 g
Protein – 3.8 g
Sodium - 19 mg

Mango Cream Pudding

Preparation Time: 10 minutes
Total Time: 4 hours 20 minutes
Yield: 6 servings

Ingredients

1 1/2 cup (375 ml) whole milk
2 (7 g) packages of plain gelatin
1 cup (250 g) mango puree
2/3 cup (165 ml) heavy cream
2/3 cup (200 ml) sweetened condensed milk
2 Tbsp. (30 ml) lemon juice
1 cup (165 g) diced mangoes

Method

1. In a small saucepan, combine the gelatin and milk. Mix well. Let sit for a minute to soften the gelatin. Cook over medium heat, stirring often until heated through and near to boiling.
2. Gradually, add the mango puree, heavy cream, condensed milk, and lemon juice. Cook, stirring for another 2-3 minutes or until heated through.
3. Pour the mixture evenly into six flan molds or ramekins and chill for at least 4 hours or until completely set.

4. Invert the molds onto serving plates. Top with diced mangoes.
5. Serve and enjoy.

Nutritional Information:
Energy - 285 calories
Fat - 9.6 g
Carbohydrates - 38.7 g
Protein - 13.9 g
Sodium - 97 mg

Almond Panna Cotta with Fresh Fruits

Preparation Time: 20 minutes
Total Time: 8 hours 20 minutes
Yield: 4 servings

Ingredients

2/3 cup (170 ml) whole milk
1 package (7 g) plain gelatin powder
2 cups (500 ml) heavy cream
1/2 cup (110 g) granulated sugar
1 tsp. (5 ml) almond extract
2 cups (300 g) fresh fruits, cut into small pieces
whipped cream, for topping

Method

1. In a small saucepan, mix together milk and gelatin. Cook over medium heat, stirring often until gelatin is fully dissolved and the mixture is heated through.
2. Stir in the cream, sugar, and almond extract. Divide equally among four heat-proof dessert cups.
3. Cover and chill for at least 8 hours or overnight. Top with some whipped cream and fresh fruits.
4. Serve immediately and enjoy.

Nutritional Information:
Energy - 353 calories
Fat - 23.3 g
Carbohydrates - 34.3 g
Protein - 4.5 g
Sodium - 46 mg

Easy Mocha Pudding

Preparation Time: 15 minutes
Total Time: 4 hours 20 minutes
Yield: 4 servings

Ingredients

2 (7 g) packages unflavored gelatin
1 cup (250 ml) whole milk
4 oz. (125 g) semisweet chocolate, melted
2 cups (500 ml) freshly brewed coffee
Chocolate chips, to serve

Method

1. Whisk together the gelatin and milk in a saucepan until dissolved.
2. Stir in melted chocolate and brewed coffee. Cook over medium flame until it simmers. Remove from heat.
3. Pour mixture equally into four flan molds or ramekins. Cool at room temperature. Cover and then chill for at least 4 hours to set.
4. Invert the molds onto serving plates. Top with some chocolate chips.
5. Serve and enjoy.

Nutritional Information:
Energy - 214 calories
Fat - 9.8 g
Carbohydrates - 20.9 g
Protein - 15.3 g
Sodium - 62 mg

Spiced Semolina Pudding with Sweet Cherries

Preparation Time: 15 minutes
Total Time: 35 minutes
Yield: 6 servings

Ingredients
1 1/2 cups (375 ml) whole milk
1 cup (250 ml) water
1 1/4 cup (275 g) white sugar
1 cinnamon stick
1/4 cup (60 g) butter
1 cup (170 g) semolina flour
Maraschino cherries, for topping

Method
1. In a medium saucepan over medium heat, mix together the milk, water, sugar, and cinnamon stick. Bring to a boil over medium-high flame. Remove from heat. Take out the cinnamon stick from the mixture and discard.
2. Melt butter in a separate saucepan over medium flame. Gradually, stir in the semolina until the mixture becomes thick and smooth.
3. Slowly add the milk mixture, stirring constantly until thick. Divide equally among six ramekins, and then top with cherries.

4. Serve warm or cold.

Nutritional Information:
Energy - 286 calories
Fat - 6.9 g
Carbohydrates - 53.1 g
Protein - 4.4 g
Sodium - 70 mg

Homemade Two Berry Semolina Pudding

Preparation Time: 15 minutes
Total Time: 2 hours 30 minutes
Yield: 8 servings

Ingredients

2 cups (400 g) fresh hulled strawberries, divided
2 cups (250 g) fresh raspberries, divided
1 cup (250 ml) water
2 cups (500 ml) whole milk
1 cup (300 ml) sweetened condensed milk
1/3 cup (85 g) butter
1 cup (170 g) semolina flour
fresh mint (for garnish)

Method

1. Place 1 cup strawberries and 1 cup raspberries in a food processor. Process until smooth. Pour in a medium saucepan.
2. Add the water, whole milk, and sweetened condensed milk. Then, bring to a boil, stirring often. Remove from heat.
3. Melt butter in another saucepan over medium heat. Slowly add the semolina, stirring constantly until the mixture is thickened.

4. Gradually, stir in the milk mixture. Cook further 3-5 minutes, stirring often until the mixture becomes smooth.
5. Divide the pudding mixture evenly among eight dessert cups or ramekins. Let cool.
6. Chill for at least 2 hours. Top with fresh berries and garnish with mint.
7. Serve and enjoy.

Nutritional Information:
Energy - 295 calories
Fat - 9.5 g
Carbohydrates - 49.7 g
Protein - 5.3 g
Sodium - 85 mg

Semolina Coconut Pudding with Raspberries

Preparation Time: 15 minutes
Total Time: 4 hours 15 minutes
Yield: 8 servings

Ingredients
1 cup (170 g) semolina flour
1/2 cup (110 g) white sugar
1/4 tsp. Kosher salt
2 cups (500 ml) skim milk
1 tsp. (5 ml) vanilla extract
1 cup (100 g) coconut flakes, divided
1 cup (250 ml) coconut milk
1 cup (125 g) fresh raspberries
fresh mint (for garnish)

Method
1. Combine the semolina, sugar, and salt in a medium saucepan. Stir in the skim milk. Cook over medium flame, stirring often until it becomes thickened. Remove from heat.
2. Add the vanilla, half of the coconut flakes, and coconut milk. Mix well and divide equally among eight dessert cups. Chill until firm, about 4 hours.

3. Top with remaining coconut flakes, fresh raspberries, and mint.
4. Serve and enjoy.

Nutritional Information:
Energy - 316 calories
Fat - 16.1 g
Carbohydrates - 40.1 g
Protein - 6.3 g
Sodium - 145 mg

Chia Yogurt and Blueberry Pudding

Preparation Time: 10 minutes
Total Time: 4 hours 20 minutes
Yield: 4 servings

Ingredients
2 cups (500 ml) skim milk
6 oz. (180 g) vanilla yogurt
3 Tbsp. (30 g) chia seeds
3 Tbsp. (60 ml) honey
2 cups (300 g) blueberries

Method
1. Mix together the milk, yogurt, chia seeds, and honey in a medium bowl. Cover and then chill for at least 4 hours to set.
2. Stir in half of the blueberries. Divide evenly among four dessert cups. Top with remaining blueberries.
3. Serve and enjoy.

Nutritional Information:
Energy - 199 calories
Fat - 3.0 g
Carbohydrates - 35.5 g
Protein - 8.2 g
Sodium - 97 mg

Chia Pudding with Matcha Pomegranates and Almonds

Preparation Time: 10 minutes
Total Time: 4 hours 20 minutes
Yield: 4 servings

Ingredients

2 cups (500 ml) almond milk, unsweetened
6 oz. (180 g) vanilla yogurt
3 Tbsp. (30 g) chia seeds
1 Tbsp. (7 g) matcha powder
3 Tbsp. (60 ml) honey
1 cup (180 g) pomegranate seeds
1/4 cup (30 g) dry roasted almonds, chopped
4 Tbsp. (30 g) Goji berries

Method

1. Mix together the milk, yogurt, chia seeds, matcha, and honey in a medium bowl until blended well. Cover and then chill for at least 4 hours to set.
2. Divide evenly among four dessert cups. Top with pomegranate seeds, almonds, and Goji berries.
3. Serve and enjoy.

Nutritional Information:
Energy - 212 calories
Fat – 7.2 g
Carbohydrates - 31.0 g
Protein – 7.6 g
Sodium - 107 mg

Coco Chia Pudding with Mango

Preparation Time: 10 minutes
Total Time: 4 hours 15 minutes
Yield: 4 servings

Ingredients

1/2 cup (125 ml) coconut milk
2 cups (500 ml) skim milk
3 Tbsp. (30 g) chia seeds
3 Tbsp. (60 ml) agave nectar
1/2 tsp. (2.5 ml) pure vanilla extract
2 cups (165 g) fresh ripe mangoes, peeled and chopped

Method

1. Mix together the coconut milk, skim milk, chia seeds, agave nectar, and vanilla extract in a medium bowl. Cover and then chill for at least 4 hours to set.
2. Stir in half of the mangoes. Divide evenly among four dessert cups. Top with remaining mangoes.
3. Serve and enjoy.

Nutritional Information:
Energy - 295 calories
Fat - 10.0 g
Carbohydrates - 47.7 g
Protein - 7.3 g
Sodium - 72 mg

Apple Cinnamon and Oat Pudding with Chia

Preparation Time: 10 minutes
Total Time: 6 hours 15 minutes
Yield: 2 servings

Ingredients

1 cup (250 ml) whole milk
6 oz. (180 g) plain Greek yogurt
1/2 cup (50 g) old-fashioned oats
1 1/2 Tbsp. (15 g) chia seeds
1/4 tsp. cinnamon, ground
1 medium (180 g) apple, cored and chopped

Method

1. Mix together the milk, Greek, yogurt, oats, chia seeds, and cinnamon in a jar or container with a tight-fitting lid. Cover and shake the mixture vigorously until combined well. Remove the lid and stir in apples. Cover and keep refrigerated for at least 6-8 hours.
2. Divide among two serving cups.
3. Serve and enjoy.

Nutritional Information:
Energy - 292 calories
Fat - 8.3 g
Carbohydrates - 39.4 g
Protein - 16.2 g
Sodium - 80 mg

Blueberry Chia Pudding with Maple

Preparation Time: 10 minutes
Total Time: 4 hours 15 minutes
Yield: 4 servings

Ingredients

2 cups (500 ml) almond milk
1/4 cup (40 g) chia seeds
2 Tbsp. (40 ml) maple syrup
1/2 tsp. (2.5 ml) pure vanilla extract
2 cups (300 g) blueberries

Method

1. Mix together the almond milk, chia seeds, maple syrup, and vanilla extract in a medium bowl. Cover and then chill for at least 4 hours to set.
2. Stir in half of the blueberries. Divide evenly among four dessert cups. Top with remaining blueberries.
3. Serve and enjoy.

Nutritional Information:

Energy - 129 calories
Fat - 4.4 g
Carbohydrates - 20.8 g
Protein - 2.9 g
Sodium - 123 mg

Strawberry and Chia Pudding with Granola

Preparation Time: 10 minutes
Total Time: 4 hours 15 minutes
Yield: 4 servings

Ingredients

2 cups (500 ml) almond milk, unsweetened
1/4 cup (40 g) chia seeds
2 Tbsp. (40 ml) honey
1/2 tsp. (5 ml) pure vanilla extract
2 cups (300 g) strawberries
1 cup (50 g) granola
whipped cream, for topping
fresh mint, for garnish

Method

1. Mix together almond milk, chia seeds, honey, and vanilla extract in a medium bowl. Cover and then chill for at least 4 hours to set.
2. Divide the granola evenly among four dessert cups. Add half of the strawberries and prepared chia pudding. Top with remaining strawberries and some whipped cream. Garnish with fresh mint.
3. Serve and enjoy.

Nutritional Information:
Energy - 176 calories
Fat - 18.3 g
Carbohydrates - 50.2 g
Protein - 11.2 g
Sodium - 93 mg

Persimmon Oat and Chia Pudding

Preparation Time: 10 minutes
Total Time: 6 hours 15 minutes
Yield: 2 servings

Ingredients

1 cup (250 ml) whole milk
6 oz. (180 g) plain Greek yogurt
1/2 cup (50 g) old-fashioned oats
2 Tbsp. (20 g) chia seeds
1 Tbsp. (20 ml) agave nectar
1 medium (150 g) persimmon, diced
fresh mint

Method

1. Mix together the milk, Greek, yogurt, oats, chia, and agave nectar, in a glass jar or container with a tight-fitting lid. Cover and shake the mixture vigorously until combined well. Cover and keep refrigerated for 6-8 hours.
2. Divide the oat-chia pudding evenly among two serving cups. Top with persimmon and garnish with fresh mint.
3. Serve and enjoy.

Nutritional Information:
Energy - 252 calories
Fat - 5.7 g
Carbohydrates - 38.4 g
Protein - 13.7 g
Sodium - 88 mg

Cardamom-Spiced Rice Pudding with Dried Cherry

Preparation Time: 10 minutes
Total Time: 25 minutes
Yield: 6 servings

Ingredients

4 cups (1 L) whole milk
2 (60 g) eggs, beaten
1/2 cup (110 g) brown sugar
1 1/2 cups (280 g) cooked white rice
1/2 cup (60 g) dried cherries
1 Tbsp. (15 g) butter
1/2 tsp. (1 g) cardamom, ground

Method

1. In a saucepan, combine the milk, eggs, brown sugar, and cooked rice. Cook over medium flame for 12-15 minutes, stirring often.
2. Stir in dried cherries, butter, and cardamom. Remove from heat.
3. Divide evenly among six individual bowls.
4. Serve warm or cold.

Nutritional Information:
Energy - 312 calories
Fat - 10.9 g
Carbohydrates - 45.6 g
Protein - 8.5 g
Sodium - 116 mg

Spiced Rice Pudding with Blueberries

Preparation Time: 10 minutes
Total Time: 25 minutes
Yield: 6 servings

Ingredients

4 cups (1 L) almond milk, unsweetened
2 (60 g) large eggs, beaten
1 1/2 cup (280 g) cooked white rice
1/2 cup (170 ml) honey
2 Tbsp. (30 g) butter
1/2 tsp. (1 g) cinnamon, ground
2 cups (300 g) blueberries

Method

1. In a saucepan, combine the almond milk, eggs, and cooked rice. Cook over medium flame for 12-15 minutes, stirring often.
2. Stir in honey, butter, cinnamon, and blueberries. Remove from heat.
3. Divide evenly among six individual bowls.
4. Serve and enjoy.

Nutritional Information:
Energy - 246 calories
Fat - 7.4 g
Carbohydrates - 42.6 g
Protein - 4.3 g
Sodium - 151 mg

Chocolate Rice Pudding with Cinnamon

Preparation Time: 10 minutes
Total Time: 25 minutes
Yield: 6 servings

Ingredients

3 1/2 cups (875 ml) low-fat milk
2 (60 g) large eggs, beaten
1/2 cup (110 g) brown sugar
1 1/2 cup (280 g) cooked white rice
3 Tbsp. (20 g) unsweetened cocoa powder
1/2 cup (125 ml) hot water
2 Tbsp. (30 g) butter
1/2 tsp. (2.5 ml) pure vanilla extract
1/2 tsp. (1 g) cinnamon, ground
whipped cream

Method

1. In a saucepan, combine the milk, eggs, brown sugar, and cooked rice. Cook over medium flame for 10-15 minutes, stirring frequently.
2. Meanwhile, combine the cocoa powder and hot water in a small bowl. Mix well until dissolved. Pour mixture into the saucepan.
3. Stir in butter and vanilla extract. Remove from the heat source.

4. Divide evenly among six dessert cups. Top with some whipped cream and sprinkle with a dash of cinnamon.
5. Serve and enjoy.

Nutritional Information:
Energy - 255 calories
Fat - 10.5 g
Carbohydrates - 32.9 g
Protein - 8.2 g
Sodium - 112 mg

Almond Rice Pudding with Figs

Preparation Time: 10 minutes
Total Time: 25 minutes
Yield: 6 servings

Ingredients

4 cups (1 L) almond milk, unsweetened
2 (60 g) large eggs, beaten
1 1/2 cup (180 g) cooked white rice
1/2 cup (160 ml) agave nectar
2 Tbsp. (30 g) butter
2 Tbsp. (15 ml) lemon juice
6 (65 g) figs, quartered
1 Tbsp. (10 g) lemon zest, finely grated

Method

1. In a saucepan, combine the almond milk, eggs, and cooked rice. Cook over medium flame for 10-15 minutes, stirring frequently.
2. Stir in agave nectar, butter, and lemon juice. Remove from the heat source.
3. Divide evenly among six individual cups. Top with figs and sprinkle with lemon zest.
4. Serve warm or cold.

Nutritional Information:
Energy - 264 calories
Fat - 7.3 g
Carbohydrates - 47.6 g
Protein - 5.0 g
Sodium - 151 mg

Mixed Berry Vanilla Rice Pudding

Preparation Time: 10 minutes
Total Time: 25 minutes
Yield: 6 servings

Ingredients

4 cups (1 L) skim milk
2 (60 g) large eggs, beaten
1 1/2 cup (180 g) cooked white rice
1/2 cup (160 ml) maple syrup
2 Tbsp. (30 g) butter
1 tsp. (5 ml) pure vanilla extract
2 cups (300 g) mixed berries

Method

1. In a saucepan, combine the milk, eggs, and cooked rice. Cook over medium flame for 10-15 minutes, stirring frequently.
2. Stir in maple syrup, butter, vanilla extract, and half of the berries. Remove from the heat source.
3. Divide evenly among six individual cups. Top with remaining mixed berries.
4. Serve warm or cold.

Nutritional Information:
Energy - 292 calories
Fat - 5.8 g
Carbohydrates - 50.4 g
Protein - 9.0 g
Sodium - 138 mg

Spiced Rice Pudding with Raisins

Preparation Time: 10 minutes
Total Time: 25 minutes
Yield: 6 servings

Ingredients

4 cups (1 L) low-fat milk
2 (60 g) eggs, beaten
1/2 cup (110 g) light brown sugar
1 1/2 cups (280 g) cooked white rice
2 Tbsp. (30 g) butter
2 tsp. (4 g) cinnamon, ground
3/4 cup (95 g) sultana raisins

Method

1. In a saucepan, combine the milk, eggs, brown sugar, and cooked rice. Cook over medium flame for 10-15 minutes, stirring frequently.
2. Stir in butter, cinnamon, and half of the raisins. Remove from the heat source.
3. Divide evenly among six individual bowls. Top with remaining raisins and sprinkle with cinnamon.
4. Serve and enjoy.

Nutritional Information:
Energy - 358 calories
Fat – 9.5 g
Carbohydrates - 57.0 g
Protein – 11.4 g
Sodium - 137 mg

Lemony Rice Pudding with Cinnamon

Preparation Time: 25 minutes
Total Time: 45 minutes
Yield: 4 servings

Ingredients

1 1/2 cups (280 g) cooked rice
2 1/2 cups (625 ml) whole milk, divided
1/2 cup (110 g) light brown sugar
1/4 tsp. Kosher salt
1 (60 g) whole egg, beaten
2 Tbsp. (30 g) butter
2 Tbsp. (30 ml) lemon juice
1 tsp. (3.5 g) lemon zest, finely grated
1 tsp. (2 g) cinnamon, ground
grated lemon rind, for garnish

Method

1. In a medium saucepan, mix together the cooked rice, 1 cup whole milk, sugar, and Kosher salt. Simmer over medium flame until creamy and thickened, about 15 minutes.
2. Stir in the remaining 1 cup of milk and beaten egg. Cook further 3 to 4 minutes, stirring frequently. Remove from heat and stir in butter, lemon juice, and zest.

3. Divide equally among four dessert cups. Sprinkle with cinnamon and garnish with lemon rind.
4. Serve warm or cold.

Nutritional Information:
Energy - 301 calories
Fat - 12.2 g
Carbohydrates - 40.3 g
Protein - 8.1 g
Sodium - 274 mg

Vanilla Rice Pudding with Warm Cherry Sauce

Preparation Time: 10 minutes
Total Time: 25 minutes
Yield: 6 servings

Ingredients

4 cups (1 L) low-fat milk
2 (60 g) eggs, beaten
1/3 cup (110 ml) agave nectar
1 1/2 cup (280 g) cooked white rice
2 Tbsp. (30 g) butter
1 tsp. (5 ml) pure vanilla extract

Warm Cherry Sauce:
2 cups (300 g) fresh cherries, pitted
1/4 cup (60 ml) port wine
1/4 cup (55 g) brown sugar
2 Tbsp. (30 ml) orange juice concentrate

Method

1. Combine the cherries, port wine, brown sugar, and orange juice concentrate in a small saucepan over medium-high flame. Bring to a boil. Lower the heat and cook further 12-15 minutes, stirring often.

2. Meanwhile, prepare the rice pudding by combining the milk, eggs, and cooked rice. Cook over medium flame for 10-15 minutes, stirring frequently.
3. Stir in agave nectar, butter, and vanilla extract. Remove from the heat source.
4. Divide evenly among six individual cups. Top with warm cherry sauce.
5. Serve and enjoy.

Nutritional Information:
Energy - 336 calories
Fat - 11.1 g
Carbohydrates - 49.9 g
Protein - 9.1 g
Sodium - 118 mg

Creamy Rice Pudding with Apple and Cinnamon

Preparation Time: 10 minutes
Total Time: 25 minutes
Yield: 6 servings

Ingredients

3 cups (750 ml) skim milk
2 (60 g) eggs, beaten
2 Tbsp. (30 ml) heavy cream
1 1/2 cup (280 g) cooked white rice
1 cup (250 g) applesauce
1/4 cup (80 ml) honey
1 tsp. (2 g) cinnamon, ground
fresh mint, for garnish

Method

1. In a saucepan, combine the milk, eggs, cream, cooked rice, and applesauce. Cook over medium flame for 10-15 minutes, stirring frequently.
2. Stir in honey, and then remove from the heat source.
3. Divide evenly among six individual cups. Sprinkle with ground cinnamon and garnish with fresh mint.
4. Serve warm or cold.

Nutritional Information:
Energy - 208 calories
Fat - 3.6 g
Carbohydrates - 36.0 g
Protein - 7.4 g
Sodium - 92 mg

Spiced Almond Rice Pudding

Preparation Time: 10 minutes
Total Time: 25 minutes
Yield: 6 servings

Ingredients

4 cups (1 L) almond milk, unsweetened
2 (60 g) eggs, beaten
1 1/2 cup (280 g) cooked white rice
2 Tbsp. (40 g) almond butter
1/2 cup (170 ml) honey
2 tsp. (4 g) cinnamon, ground
1/2 cup (60 g) dry roasted almonds, chopped
cinnamon sticks, for garnish

Method

1. In a saucepan, combine the milk, eggs, cooked rice, almond butter, and cinnamon. Cook over medium flame for 10-15 minutes, stirring frequently.
2. Stir in honey, and then remove from the heat source.
3. Divide evenly among individual bowls. Sprinkle with chopped almonds.
4. Garnish with cinnamon sticks, if desired.
5. Serve warm or cold.

Nutritional Information:
Energy - 269 calories
Fat - 10.4 g
Carbohydrates - 40.2 g
Protein - 6.8 g
Sodium - 125 mg

Yummy Orange Pudding

Preparation Time: 15 minutes
Total Time: 1 hour 15 minutes
Yield: 8 servings

Ingredients

4 (20 g) egg yolks
4 (40 g) egg whites
1/4 cup (60 ml) orange juice concentrate
2 Tbsp. (30 g) unsalted butter
3/4 cup (165 g) granulated sugar
3/4 cup (90 g) all-purpose flour, sifted
1/4 tsp. (1.5 g) Kosher salt
1 3/4 cups (440 ml) whole milk
hot water
powdered sugar, for dusting

Method

1. Preheat your oven and set it to 350 F (175 C).
2. Combine the egg yolks, orange juice concentrate, and unsalted butter together in a large bowl and mix until it thickens.
3. In a separate bowl, combine the sugar, all-purpose flour, and Kosher salt.
4. Add the dry mixture alternately with milk to the yolk mixture. Mix until blended well.

5. Beat the egg whites until stiff, and then fold in egg whites into the prepared batter.
6. Pour pudding mixture into eight ramekins. Place them into a large baking pan, then gently pour hot water into the pan to cover about half an inch. Put the baking pan in the oven and bake for 1 hour. Let cool on a wire rack.
7. Dust with some powdered sugar before serving.
8. Enjoy.

Nutritional Information:
Energy - 279 calories
Fat - 9.4 g
Carbohydrates - 41.8 g
Protein - 8.2 g
Sodium - 181 mg

Sweet Lemon Pudding Cake

Preparation Time: 15 minutes
Total Time: 1 hour
Yield: 6 servings

Ingredients

4 (20 g) egg yolks
4 (40 g) egg whites
1/4 cup (60 ml) lemon juice
1 tsp. (3.5 g) lemon zest, finely grated
2 Tbsp. (30 g) unsalted butter
1 cup (220 g) granulated sugar
2/3 cup (80 g) all-purpose flour, sifted
1/4 tsp. (1.5 g) Kosher salt
2 cups (500 ml) whole milk
hot water
powdered sugar, for dusting

Method

1. Preheat your oven and set it to 350 F (175 C).
2. Mix the egg yolks, lemon juice, lemon zest, and unsalted butter together until it thickens.
3. In a separate bowl, combine the sugar, all-purpose flour, and Kosher salt. Add this mixture alternately with milk to the yolk mixture. Mix well.

4. Beat the egg whites until stiff. Fold in egg whites into prepared mixture.
5. Divide the pudding mixture evenly among six ramekins and place them into a large baking pan. Pour hot water into the pan to cover about half an inch. Put the baking pan in the oven and bake for 40 to 45 minutes or until tested done. Let cool on a wire rack.
6. Dust with some powdered sugar before serving.
7. Enjoy.

Nutritional Information:
Energy - 308 calories
Fat - 9.8 g
Carbohydrates - 48.5 g
Protein - 8.4 g
Sodium - 187 mg

Bread Pudding with Cranberry and Caramel Sauce

Preparation Time: 15 minutes
Total Time: 1 hour 35 minutes
Yield: 8 servings

Ingredients
1 (14 oz. or 397 ml) can sweetened condensed milk
4 (60 g) whole eggs, lightly beaten
1 1/4 cups (315 ml) hot water
1/4 cup (60 g) butter, melted
1 tsp. (5 ml) pure vanilla extract
1 tsp. (2 g) cinnamon, ground
1/2 tsp. (1 g) nutmeg, ground
1 (8 oz. or 250 g) French bread, cut into small cubes
2 cups cranberries
cooking oil spray

Easy Caramel Sauce:
1/2 cup (150 g) condensed milk
1/4 cup (60 g) butter
2 Tbsp. (40 ml) light corn syrup

Method
1. Preheat your oven and set it to 320 F (160 C). Grease a 9x13-inch baking dish with oil spray.

2. Combine the sweetened condensed milk and the eggs in a large mixing bowl. Stir in hot water, butter, vanilla, cinnamon, and nutmeg.
3. Add the French bread and cranberries into the egg mixture until the bread is completely soaked.
4. Transfer the bread pudding mixture into the prepared baking dish.
5. Bake in the oven for about an hour or until a skewer inserted in the center comes out clean.
6. Meanwhile, prepare the caramel sauce by mixing together the sweetened condensed milk, 1/4 cup butter, and corn syrup in a saucepan. Bring to a boil over medium heat. Reduce heat to a simmer and cook further 10 minutes or until just slightly thickened. Let cool slightly.
7. Remove the bread pudding from the oven. Allow to cool slightly before serving, about 10 minutes.
8. Serve the bread pudding warm drizzled with caramel sauce.

Nutritional Information:
Energy - 342 calories
Fat - 12.8 g
Carbohydrates - 47.2 g
Protein - 9.6 g
Sodium - 232 mg

Bread Pudding with Raisins and Walnuts

Preparation Time: 15 hours
Total Time: 1 hour 35 minutes
Yield: 8 servings

Ingredients

1 (14 oz. or 397 ml) can sweetened condensed milk
3 (60 g) whole eggs, lightly beaten
1 1/4 cups (315 ml) hot water
1/4 cup (60 g) butter, melted
1 tsp. (5 ml) pure vanilla extract
1 tsp. (2 g) cinnamon, ground
1 (8 oz. or 250 g) French bread, cut into small cubes
2/3 cup (80 g) seedless raisins
1/2 cup (50 g) walnuts, coarsely chopped
cooking oil spray

Method

1. Preheat your oven and set it to 320 F (160 C). Grease a 9x13-inch baking dish with oil spray.
2. Mix together the sweetened condensed milk and the eggs in a large mixing bowl. Stir in hot water, butter, vanilla extract, and cinnamon.
3. Add the French bread, raisins, and walnuts into the egg mixture until the bread is completely soaked.

4. Transfer the bread pudding mixture into the prepared baking dish.
5. Bake in the oven for 1 hour or until a skewer inserted in the center comes out clean.
6. Remove the pudding from the oven. Allow to cool slightly before serving, about 10 minutes.
7. Enjoy.

Nutritional Information:

Energy - 342 calories

Fat - 12.8 g

Carbohydrates - 47.2 g

Protein - 9.6 g

Sodium - 232 mg

Thanks a lot!

I hope you enjoyed making all the recipes here.

For more great tasting recipes, please check out my other titles on Amazon.

Made in United States
North Haven, CT
28 September 2024

57966735R10065